NOCTURNAL SPARK

SARAH SAROSH

This book is dedicated to:

My Parents: Sadaf Usman and Sarosh Khawar

&

My Husband: Saif F. Mahamood

Contents

Contents

Acknowledgements

I express my utmost gratitude to Allah SWT for His infinite blessings. I would also like to thank my parents for their prayers and constant support.

I owe my Siblings for their encouragement and motivation in all my accompolishmets and goals .

READERS,

I HOPE YOU RELATE TO THIS...

1. THE MIGHTIEST SWORD

Proclaiming the rippling words of man,
Invading the realm of highest spheres,
Penning the woes of every tongue
That turns human lips to Iyers,
A sword that sharpens with rising pain of endurance,
Gift of Pen to the mankind you bestowed,
Which is only a fragment of Ultimate sword,
That you claim within thine Sovereign hold.
Using that very chipped piece
To you I make complaint
O Lord heed to my plaintive voice,
That with humble heart I raise!
Grace the action of your Mightiest sword of Justice,
To end the catastrophe
Now that viruses rule human lives,
And your Earth is losing it's divinity.
Isin't it high time to shower upon us your mercy?!

2. SO WHAT IS TIME...?

Time is a capricipous being!
Its a soothing ally to hurtful days and a seething rival to moments of bliss
But what is it to a heart of memories, mixed?
Cannot some events be serendipitous in their sense
But simultaneously sinister?
Cannot some people prove inconspicuous appetency
Of conscience but also a constant prick to emotions?
Aren't some feelings beautiful but fills you with regret?
And some stories be complete, without really an End?
So what is Time to those times of irony at its best?!

3. O FOREIGNER..

O foreigner, stop here, thee
For a little while bear with me
This bare skin lacks human touch
And long since enchanteur, I see
Imprtisoned in royalty
Ascribed a novel sublimity
Forbidden of the elixir o' love
I raise in patience my posterity.
But wonderment exclaim at times
As desire fills each artery
to admire the godly quintessence
iIwish to transgress my boundary.
Then pricks me to death, conscirence
So hold back,I, my modesty
Enshroud under wealthy riches
I lose my transiennt identity.
Alas! rekindles Leila's passion
When eyes revel upon a beauty
So bear with me for some time
O foreigner, stop here, thee
O foreigner, stop here, thee

4. INDEED THE HELP IS NEAR..

Palestine is the region of great Islamic significance, 7th century onwards. Being the third holiest and most prestigious sites, AL- AQSA mosque, has been a dome of Muslim allegiance to their roots and dispute with Israeli power over decades.

Commending the valour and gallant demeanour to fray with the opposition, the stanzas mirror motivational ideas encrypted in inspirational concept.

Thwarting the valiance of fiery souls
Holding ammunitions, They stand
But those who pray under the shade of swords
Never lose their stance.
Glorious Kalma(faith) on tongues, in sajdah(prostration) they fall
Before the Almighy, The Sovereign
Then ,let not scare them, the oppression of disbelievers
For They'll(oppressors) soon meet their ends.
The day my Lord has promised,
The hour that will befall
Just bide the Resurrection
And the blow of Final Call
They'll capture the entire domain
And take over Aqsa Mosque,
To direct the world at their whims

Yet deter will not the Momin's(pious and noble) taqwa(faith)
Across avalanche of hardships, he'll swim
And Moses victory over Pharoah of Egypt
What makes them forget?
Solomon's rule, Abraham's truth
The One message of every Prophet.
But keep patience O Palestinians
Verily Allah is all aware
We'll pass this trial with belief upright
To the day when in utter horror they'll(oppressoprs) stare
When no help will come to them
And they'll come forth abashed
When their misdeeds will weigh Them down
And the Hellfire will turn them into ash
So fray with all might and do not be steered
With you, Palestinians, is all mankind
Indeed Allah's help is near..

5. AYE HOLD ONTO YOUR BREATH..

Aye hold on to your breath my Martyr
Hold onto your breath.
You've won your battle right
For a moment see your nation's pride
Seek the glory of thy exulant army
Before venturing into the skies
Let thy vision acquire the homage of your flag
;et salvation twinkle in your eyes!
Resounding the accent of your anthem
Thrilling spires of victory on lands
Extended your domain in West,
And claimed thy honour on African Sands
Clunk of passion trembles not your senses?
Or have you forgotten your allegiance?
Then what makes you hoist White,
capitulating in the Battle of life?
The world vouch for thy courageous fight
For a moment see your nation's pride..
Aye hold onto your breath my Martyr
Hold onto your breath.

6. THE OCEAN WORLD

The mystic blue in wavy convulse
Secured habitat of thousands
Bed of silt, treasured grit
With majestic aura on the surface.
Solemn quiet, ocean bright
iIs demeanour screams- perfect!
Sparkling white, reflecting light
Whispers to a sailor, of serenity
in it's own dialect.
Angry it not, for it
Roars of catrastrophe,
When enraged.
Clutching millions in its grasp
This mightu creation
even engulfed the Titanic.
Sinister enveloped down
The layers deep
The trenches so thick,
Forbids sunrays underneath
Deemed as its deepest horizon
Is where the devil sleeps.

7. THE UNEQUIVOCAL BOUNTY

From the old recollection's hand, auto account of the most serendipitious events, noted in articulate manner of the Wedding sequence of 20th March 2022.

I

The heart knows no better place
Than the White on the table, that's neatly laid
To resign its vehemence of audacious yester
That records the sublime decree of My Master!
For the one sparing a glance at the sheet
Shall be a witness to the mirth of this Daughter of Eve
Whose fonts trace the spark in her veins
That reigns her soul's indelible zeal.
Ye question of course for such heyhey
To a heeding ear, it's thine right
And I promise to not let thee despair
Or despoil thee of thy precious time
Now from some vivid recollection's hands
The grail of ecstacy flow
Dating back to 20th March
When the visage reflected a different glow.
When my fingers impelled to sign a bond
That ties one in wedlock

Under the glorious shade of everyone's blessing
From 'Shalimar',the palanquin rose.

II

And danced in joy
The ramparts of the sky
Should I praise the invention of Edison
Or was the moon more luminous that night?
Then the 'Blossoms' walls lock in them
The fun and laughter games
That raptured from the Young souls
In heightened sense of enjoyment.
Soon the calls from vales of Kannur
Danced and thrilled in glee
Summoned us to its pilgrimage
To revel in- God's Own Country!
The dusk of 25th then
Holds a special credit of mention
As no night ever passed like
The night before Reception
Not that I will ever forget
The gleaming eyes of my dear ones
When the anecdotes resurfaced
From underneath the heavy blankrt of dust

III

26th welcomed with it,
Quintessential celebration
That never crossed my
Poor mind's farthest imagination.
Set amid the brightest diadem

Was the stage where I royally sat
Crooning to the melodious tunes
That raised from 'Arab sands'
Filling the world in sparkle
Festooned with gems I sashayed
To capture the moments and
Cut the cake, across the table, that was placed.
Alas! the orb of day got tired
And night's glory retired
As my pen seek mercy too
I pause the tale and bid adieu..

8. CONFIDING IN SELF

Invigorating passion boils in my theme of eloquence
When naked thoughts despoil the agony of my heart
The foul play of a Friend, let not drown my eyes
As lamentation is a sign of death in the Battle of Life
Nay, dispose no figment of imagination
Is a learned lesson in years
For adavantage over the,bestows, thy tongue
To ther one listening with thirtsy ears.
Gallant is not a soul reigning kingdoms
But confiding in self, supreme and sufficient
At the point of dagger of belief you fray
And armour will be thy conscience
Conspire against thee
One who'll bear your morrow pursuit
Success awaits, hold fast your dreams, if you..

9. LIFE OF A RAG-PICKER

I gaze out of my window, notice
A soul burdened of bags
Wandering across streets, in search of rags
Arduous a task it is, proves
The glistening sweat, trickling
Down his back
Pensive I get seeing him
Day in and out slog
The shreds he collects is not trash
Every piece has a story attached
But under the blazing sun
As he strive for the day's fund
Might his soul ever realize that?

10. REAL PANDEMIC

Obnoxious condition of Corona Outbreak in 2019, the most dreaded pandemic on the humankind, brought the entire world to a halt. Amid this helter skelter, Uttar Pradesh, in North of India, faced immense crowd rushing to religious site of Kumbh fair, owing to political tactics of evoking religious sentiments in public to gain central power, unfortunately averting eyes from the fatal consequences.

Wan and wane, the mindset now dwells
Over the running lines of boredom and pain
Busy, yet not
Present, but not
Life has come to what stage?
Cruel animosity of wisdom in leaders
Has pushed us to the verge of desperate ends
Pandemic was and a Pandemic is
But of folly more than what Corona rends.
Belief of purification by sacred drops of Ganges
To the fair of Kumbh invited thousands
And met they, accursed destiny, with early demise
Ah! ludicrous was their wit and judgement.
Then elections and rallies for a Winning party
Was not to be compromisdd but much held
So what if commoners deal with the disease
Aye power is important huh?!
Damn the statistics.

Already been a year, caged in the house
But the lockdown doesn't cease to extend
Helter skelter every soul of Uttar Pradesh
Now lives in a terrored state again.
Roads and skies have been abandoned
Rampant is the living despair
When rested from profanities on tongues
Mouths celebrate the Economic mayhem.
Then you ask me of my wellness?
Worry not, I am safe.
If safe is the definition of dubious, lugubrious silence
Verily, I am the Safest of the Safe..

11. THREE STEPS OF LIFE

That First cry of baby into a new world
Where it first exercises it's lungs
And is new to the open air
Where it's choice, if given, would be in
Womb to remain.
Then it feels a comfotring touch
An anonymous bond thus, created on Earth
Unconditional love, reflecting mother's mirth
Her heavenly smell that connects heart to heart
When in world of darkness, instinct plays the part.
Lapse of time leads to the first agonizing
Fear of departure for both
Merely for three hours,
When the child, for the first time
Independently crosses the threshold of domestic setup
From the world outside of mother's womb
Then outside Her arms
To a very foreign world
Tearing them apart.
As the child grows, Mother olds
Their distance expands and rends
Difficulty in bridging both ends..

12. PLEA OF UNION

O hear- The rising ocean waves
Tell my sailor of my winter days
My bosoms heaves the loss of
His tender touch and passionate kiss
O hear- The rising ocean waves.
O burnt up boughs and Autumn gales
How frequently your seasons change
Those silver strands on my forehead
Are witness to the boring age
I spent without his arms' cage
O burnt up boughs and Autumn gales
Aye loo of Summer on Arabian Sands
Of my sailor's address are you aware?
Or your merry tunes were in artistic travail
To have missed the radiance of his stare,
And not forward my plea of union
That got lost in loop of time's hands
Aye loo of Summer on Arabian Sands.
Ahem, The Tropical air
Nay I do not plead to hear from you
Any news of my beloved
For I fear the presence of him above skies
Is my cue to know that he is dead
So return to your abode where

In ultimate bliss the spirits rest
Lo I do not plead to hear from you
Nay o nay ..The Tropical air.

13. AN EVENING DRINK WITH MY ENEMY

The quintessence of vengeance
Twinkled in the beads of his eyes
Wearing the kohl of spite,
He measured each of his lies.
His impassive countenance welcomed
When I proffered a ceasefire
‘Cause perhaps the lack of sincerity
In my invite was quite obvious
Old accounts offered the reminiscence of scenes,
Recalled the last of our bitter memories
’Romeo‘ better than a ’Hobbes' he was
Love was mightier than our friendship indeed.
By the perils of life,
Through mires of jeopardy,
What afflicted our bond
Faced affront our fury
But now we roll our eyes in mutual wrath
Alas this was the destination to our journey
From the cheers in his name
To the table onto which now I share-
An Evening Drink With My Enemy.

14. FREEDOM

I would like to rise and go
Where people live freely and grow.
Where there will be no inequality
And the hearts will be free and sprightly.
Where poor will not be enslaved
And soft-heartneres will not be rare.
Where everyone will live with harmony
To promote Justice and Peace.
Let the spirits never die
Still we can fly up high.
We won't let anyone rule us
Now it's time to stand in unison.
We have all rights to live freely
Even we have our dignity.
So leave the life of slavery
And change your dreams to reality.
Yes!.. we've got to get free.

15. THE RAINBOW LIFE

Indeed beauteast thou, colours of the sky
Tearing through the dark dense clouds
Reflecting the delectation of someone abiding
Beyond the heavens, in glory, enshroud.
But to the beck of my thoughts, I oblige, with zeal
Riding across the silent woods, as I salve myself in thy ecstacy
erring by transgressing ,thou compare
On the ground, to the mortal specks of clay.
Violet and Indigo turns shade over head on dreary days
Standing proud in raiment green,
Trees eye the tides and blue waves
Their legions convert orange upon season's change
And yellow streaks dance in the petals of daffodils
But Red, the symbol of luxuriance reign
As the desire o' love flows in
Leila Majnu's veins
Lo thus, Rainbow is life, not I lie
Indeed beauteast thou, colours of the sky!

16. SENECTITUDE

The finger thou so reliably entwine with thine,
One day, decrepit will be.
The steps you compete to match up,
Will taste the dish of debility.
Encumberant, my limbs, on the bed legs
Then shall retire permanently
To the day my sepulchre will anticipate
Of me with appetency.
O lad, so will you not reason with my senectitude
With my senectitude, not reason, will you?
Alert thou I, of my, adding age
Soon will reach my last stage
Leaving a series of nostalgic moments
As a legacy to my lineage
Wan to wane-
Wan to wane, I will
O lad, so will you not reason with my senectitude
With my senectitude, not reason, will you?
Senility sure, shall mark my account of demeanour
And today where you sit- around my neck
Time will droop those shoulders.
One day this parsonage that I grandly build too
Will just enclose me in a room of little honour.
O lad, so will you not reason with my senectituide

With my senectitude, not reason ,will you?
Ha! Fright not Young Muscles
In my latter phase I will be fine
Wont even trouble your ears with my incessant cries
Though secretly wish that you'd buy some time
If not for me, then to visit my shrine..

17. DISARRAYED WILDLIFE

O black striped animal,
In all your might you walk
Eyes so dense and poised
You catch your prey
And roves your balls.
Your roar terrifies the jungle
And mountains tremble with fright
When you summon the creatures
Even the birds descend from heights.
Tiger- they call you by name
The crown of jungle you wear
With your royal demeanour
Even Royalty, you put to shame
But few of your kind remains now,
Gracing the Earth
And sumptuous your skin
Adorns the abode of us.
Thus mourns your extinct
A disarray Wildlife
As You have deserted your throne
By your demise..

18. IF I WERE A SCIENTIST

Beirut Explosion- On 4 August 2020, Ammonium Nitrate compound, stored at Beirut Port in Lebanon ,exploded, causing thousands to die tragically and leaving others homeless. Mourning the loss, poet ponders over the significance of life and challenges scientists to defy death.

I may not know of Technology and Science,
But well acquainted I am to the essence of life.
'Embryology' and 'Mitosis', intrigue me not, sure
Though undulated wrinkles on the-
visage of my Mother reflects what?
That I am well aware of.
If the atoms and molecules fused unto galaxy
or Big Bang led to forming orbs and universe
But bother of it, I, less compared
To the reason behind Beirut explosion.
Nay I care not of' Anatomy' or 'Geology'
Or of chemical reactions in acids and bases
But the rising levels of Global Warming,
And its effects on creatures leaves me dazed.
'Pollination' and 'Germination' tell me not much of them,
'Cause I am a listener of the woes of wildlife disarrayed
You study 'Reproduction' and I study their cries
Hence I am a scientist better in grade

But let me out a secret from my chest
That my mind and heart constantly bicker
If I were a scientist, what all I could change
Unravel mysteries and bring revolution.
Doth plead my conscience, I am not one
From the knowledge of Science, I far lie
Yet I strive to discover the significance of life
And so the defendant doth that plead deny!

19. THAT BEAUTY IN YELLOW

Crispy scrunch of Autumn petals
Or the Sun's golden hue with tinted lemon
The antique floral pigment of sunflowers and daffodils
Each reflect 'Yellow' in itself.
The shiny streak of rainbow lines
Or the essence of marine life
Glitteringf even in the wings of butterfly
Is the very yellow, divine.
To the brightest diadem it belongs
Surrealism ,it's the epitome, of
Nature of felicitry comes with it
When code yellow in eyes, hit.
From the gay buds of garden hymns,
A songster hears the yellow delights
To the tiny flickers in fireflies
It's beauty reigns great heights!

20. WOE TO DESTINY

At the procession of thy beauty
Time intends a zealous pilgrimage to thee
There embrace thy lineament, I
Yet not feel guilty.
Woe to destiny
Lovers then not lovers now
Beholder of your soul once
My heart doth plead thy heart, a vow
Torment me not by the glittering shimmer,
And the infidel spark in eyes
Nor convoluted promises
Failing to live for lifetime
It's your lover's vehemence after all
That has conceived such conceit
But proud doth not on thyself
Or let affectation, thy innocence steal..

21. INCONSPICUOUS REALITY

Behind the curtains of decency
Some illicit affairs rest
Under the shade of nobility
Thrives the evil pests
And what gives you the idea
That Goodness is always returned?
Lo! from the most dazzling eyes
Tears of beytrayal sheds...

22. BEAUTY IN THE BEAUTY

M world spins, coating each nerve with ecstacy
When the rays of sun reflects on you
I see heaven in my eyes
When I compliment you,
Those cheekbones rise
That blush on your face
And the adrenaline rush in my veins
Is beyond the realm of words
Yet I take the pain
To capture you on this page..

23. ODE TO MANGO

Has not my sweetness, enchanted thine tongue?
Myriad flavours combined in one.
When thine dripping sweat would woe under the sun
And demand a taste of mango pulp!
The harvest breathes demise at my presence
I reign the symbol opf luxuriance
Hath I been a barbaric fruit King
Would still the knife's ordeal, I bear?
Nectar to a parched throat
Electrifying every nerve end
With delicacy I would pour myself
To meet your relishimg sense.
Then seek for me in June and July
From scorching heat, to rescue self of thy
Bide the time of my advent
And I'll be sweeter far then.

24. REFLECTION OF PAST

I wrapped myself in the garb of despondence
Wallowed over my fate to the Sovereign
The demise of my dear, had left me distraught
That over days, my agony, I couldn't end.
Cult of emotions screamed for mercy
And one night, the dark chest of slumber,
Captured me in its sanctuary-
Clasping my hand in its impalpable touch
My reflection came to visit me.
A message it whispered in my ears,
Stirred my conscience to life
Said- latch up the doors of Past forever
And to find the key to Future, thou strive
Mortal is every being on planet
Its just the Game of Time..

25. MY VILLAGE

My day's travail, permit not my limbs, to be at ease
But that crescent moon undersatnds my plea
Slumber consent not, my droopy eyes to meet thee
Thus you're summoned, in arid land of my dreams
Sneaking out from the Heaven's arms,
At ungodly hours
Then gently, would kiss the surface of my planet
Succumbing to the Sun, larks would endeavour their search
Would then every soul, lament over their despoiled blankets.
Trees stand proud of their raiment
Augmenting thy royalty,
Songster would sing,
Unmoved by change of seasons
In the arms of its beauty.
Cattle bred and farmers, gey at harvest
Rejoice their retire, at dusk, to home returnest
Every hour, was to us mortals, festival
At times, the sky would weep of mirth
Such was my village.
Alas! by day, my body and by night, my mind
Would remind me of that paradise, existing once upn a time
Never abandoned I would have, the sublime creation of Almighty
Hadst thou not entrapped me in fallacy of Urban colonies
Cursed me the woes of creatures under the soil

Above I lie, beneath, their dead bodies..

26. LETTER OF DESPAIR

I raised you when you were abandoned
And cared for you with all my passion
I treated you the best in every way
If only I knew, you'd go astray
I seemed hurtful to you when you were young
Those little Lies that you had on your tongue
The times I had to be strict to inculcate manners
And others when I was sweet to make you finer.
Now you have grown and I am alone
Nobody in the world appears to me known
My Prime days seems to have flown
Are you there or even you are gone?
My only demand is more of your affection
Why in our relation, is there so much a tension?
I expected for myself a special position
Or maybe I am expecting a lot
Is it something you can't afford?

27. A COMIC MORNING

I wake up at 6 in the morning
My dishevelled state, in every direction, stumbling
I pull my feet out of the blanket
And stand in front of mirror to gaze
What I see is not likely to my taste
For I encounter my drooling face!
It's 6:15 and I have worn my pants
Now where is my shirt?
What is it doing under the cuupboard?
I'll wear a tie and get set to go
What?! why is it tied to my shoes in a bow?
My socks are nowhere in sight
My my! who kept them in freezer all night?
Car keys should be in pocket
In pocket of my wallet
And the last I saw of it was-
On the seat of my Toilet.
Now is time for breakfast of cereal and rice
Weird combo?
'Cause I am not Mr.Right.
Phew! I am finally ready
And it's time to head out
Oh, but I bear a doubt
The calendar reads- 24th may

No way..Is it Sunday?!

28. PROMISE TO SELF

Impregnable to thy charm
I guard my eyes from falling on foreign beauty
Now, neither anymore, claim my right on you, I
Nor invite you to my abode of dreams.
Submerged under the blanket of time
Moments of our togetherness rests
And when the gust of past blows
Its exposed to the whiff of nostalgic air
Alas, in garden that lies shorn
A songster sits and all day mourn
But only if there were some in there
To feel the burden of it's moan.
You'd grace my morning slumbers
Gleam such that even diamonds shame
Past it is and a past so-
That I lock this Trunk forever
With an intention to never recall your name.

29. IN THE BOLOVIAN LAND

In the trench of Bolovian land, abided a restless soul
With nocturnal cries it would wake up all
Silhouetting by the Full moon.
And every implacable heart shall solicit mysteriously
The cause of the bootless cries
Of what agony it behold
But the unkempt occassions of encounter
And ill bearing of calls
Failed to deliver to kids, the story behind midnight howls.
Then wIth intended zeal and quest of honour
I walked into the eerie deep woods
Fiery valour laced in the armour of suit
My affectation vowed me the victory hoot
For a thousand years in the silky ripples
The oceans reported no such being
imod the Green, beyond the Blues
Even the air was all serene.
The laboured swerat criod out in woe
And I hath to redeem
Alas, again the fortnight of the last December
Mirriored me to me
Pained of unrequired saga, some true love, the voices beseeched

Just claimed by none other than my own human skinned beast.

30. A DREAMY DREAM

A windy night sure it was
That swept my soul away
To the land of Ecstacy
On a one horse riding sleigh.
To The Garden of Eden
With paved rosebed
and a golden angelic halo
Over every creature's head
Exquisite layers of beauty
In wonders of extravagance
A familiar face, I see
Royally throned and dressed
Grapes and wine, nine dishes to die
How beautiful I looked in the Claok of Paradise!
Alas, The splash of cold water
And a call of- Rise and Shine!

31. PLEA OF UNION

Against the venom of social decency
And the rampant surge of antipathy
The will of promising notion o' love
My heart shall soon find in thee.
Yeah I may not be the right one for you
Or it just may not be the right time
But wrong is good and good is you
All the rest is fallacy!
You come to me today or wait for tomorrow
no plaint shall I bear despite this agony
But promise to come and come back soon
So that in passage of time
I lose you not, nor you lose me..

32. DEADLIER THAN ACID

Yes I am ugly.. Yes I am ill-fated
Yes iI am broken wondering if I deserve hatred.
Why are my relations all severed after I returned from hospital bed?
They say the answer lies in morroi
But looking into it, is what I dread.
My reflection would encounter me to the harsh reality
To the scars on my face and burns on body
I am aware that this curse will never end
but it filtered my foes who were camouflaged as friends
Is it my fault that I was the Victim?
'Cause victim I was and not the Culprit.
Heartless mistake me not
To be impregnable to abhorrence
Sure God showed me that sometimes
Humans are be deadlier than acid.

33. MANSION OF DEATH

One sinister night unfolded the inconspicuous
Fright in my bones.
The shrill clamour deafened my ears,
The teary bloodshot eye smooched my skin,
And I throated down each breath with fear.
Curse be to 32nd April
The date of their demise
Erased from the pages of calendar
Yet locking their souls, inspite
Sweat beads trickle down my forehead
And lungs threaten to push out air
But to escape these immortal spirits
Of the slightest sound, I must beware.
To lock in this mansion of death
My fate conspired againsty me
Acceptoing their cordial invite
I traded my life, unknowingly..

34. I LET GO OF YOU

You asked me how I look at you, I kept mum
You asked what I think of you, I stifled my inner voice
I was beading a chain of memories wherein
Piddling in the unsultry manner, your hair
Would entertain themselves on my face
And with knitted brows, you tame them
When your cheekbones lifted everytime you smiled at me,
I would take a secret flight to a galaxy ,undiscovered
The tips of your smooth skin would graze by my stubble
Tugging the hurricane of emotions
But when the whiff of my admiration ,whispered in your ears
And a soft slap of reality balanced my senses
I let go of you
still keeping my silence..

35. TWIST

Turning across the ebbs of dreams
I narrowed my desires of achievements and hopes
Will the life provide better opportunities?
A voice questions through the soul.
Lest, I circumspect ill changes
The devastated self will remain ever so
Mires of feelings tangles of fate
Will keep me entrapped in my monotonous role.
Hence,
A twist in route, a twist in plan
A twist in destination on map
A twist in me, a twist in you
Will resweeeten the memories blue
So bring about the wondrous change
Let's shake our bellies to Life's Twisted tune!

36. ET TU BRUTE?!

No words to speak
No emotions to feel
There's silence that surrounds
And open scars that will never heal.
I am lost within myself
And there's nobody to trust
Life's a pain
And heart, too, hurts
It's dark within me
I am dead inside
No more the energy,
No guts to fight.
Avalanche of voices screams within
losing my identity, I am breaking in
I wish that I could go, free to be myself
I reach out for a hand
But there's nobody to lend.
When betrayed by a friend,
Smiles can be feigned, Aye.
Yet lips impassively utter
'Et tu Brute..?!'

37. REFLECTION OF ME

Knitted brows decors your countenance
Yet I catch your balls on the periphery of your eyes
Trying to steal a glimpse of me, oblivious-
To the fact, not for a moment have you left my sight
And even if for a fraction of second
But a moment is recorded as-
'The Reflection Of Me In Your Eyes..'

38. ROME WASN'T BUILT IN A DAY

When your limbs give in to the travails of world
And every bone shrieks in pain
Vision of success haze in time
Or negativity fill your brain.
Then bear in mind that every task demands
Your sweat and blood as a pay
So give up not to obtacles
Remember- Rome Wasn't built In A Day!

Printed by Libri Plureos GmbH in Hamburg,
Germany